To Celebrate

_____

_____

Date

_____

THANK YOU FOR COMING.

Let's celebrate!

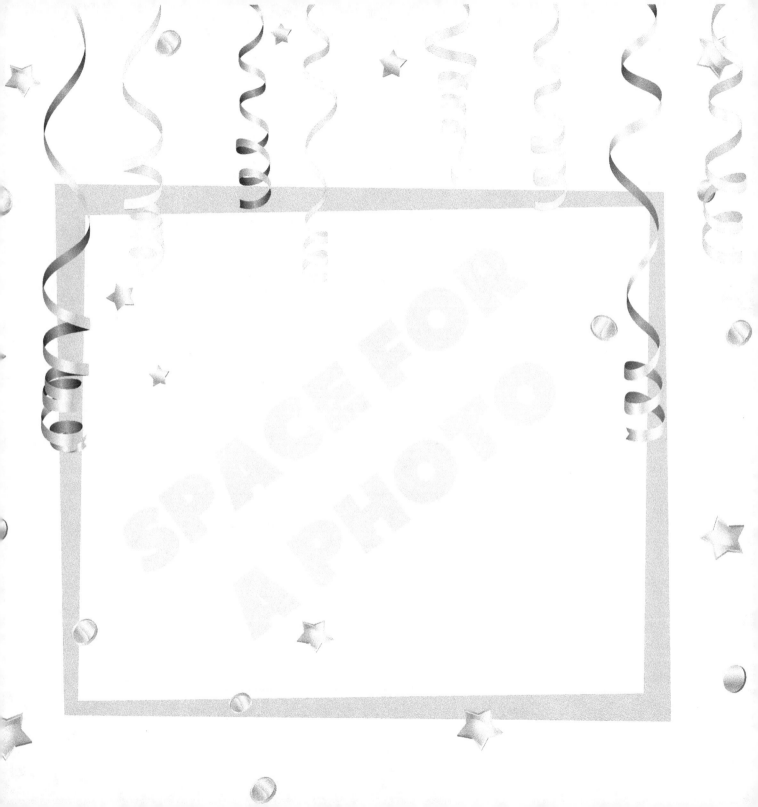

Guest Name

_____

Wishes & Messages

_____

_____

_____

_____

_____

_____

_____

EMAIL/PHONE

Guest Name

_____

Wishes & Messages

_____

_____

_____

_____

_____

_____

_____

Email/Phone

Guest Name

_____

Wishes & Messages

_____

_____

_____

_____

_____

_____

_____

Email/Phone

Guest Name

_____

Wishes & Messages

_____

_____

_____

_____

_____

_____

_____

Email/Phone

Guest Name

_____

Wishes & Messages

_____

_____

_____

_____

_____

_____

_____

Email/Phone

Guest Name

_____

Wishes & Messages

_____

_____

_____

_____

_____

_____

_____

✉ E

Email/Phone

Guest Name

_____

Wishes & Messages

_____

_____

_____

_____

_____

_____

_____

Email/Phone

Guest Name

_____

Wishes & Messages

_____

_____

_____

_____

_____

_____

EMAIL/PHONE

Guest Name

_____

Wishes & Messages

_____

_____

_____

_____

_____

_____

✉ E

EMAIL/PHONE

Guest Name

_____

Wishes & Messages

_____

_____

_____

_____

_____

_____

_____

Email/Phone

Guest Name

_____

Wishes & Messages

_____

_____

_____

_____

_____

_____

Email/Phone

Guest Name

_____

Wishes & Messages

_____

_____

_____

_____

_____

_____

_____

EMAIL/PHONE

Guest Name

_____

Wishes & Messages

_____

_____

_____

_____

_____

_____

_____

✉ E

Email/Phone

Guest Name

_____

Wishes & Messages

_____

_____

_____

_____

_____

_____

Email/Phone

Guest Name

_____

Wishes & Messages

_____

_____

_____

_____

_____

_____

_____

Email/Phone

Guest Name

_____

Wishes & Messages

_____

_____

_____

_____

_____

_____

✉ E

EMAIL/PHONE

Guest Name

_____

Wishes & Messages

_____

_____

_____

_____

_____

_____

_____

Email/Phone

Guest Name

_____

Wishes & Messages

_____

_____

_____

_____

_____

_____

✉ Email/Phone

Guest Name

_____

Wishes & Messages

_____

_____

_____

_____

_____

_____

Email/Phone

Guest Name

_____

Wishes & Messages

_____

_____

_____

_____

_____

_____

_____

EMAIL/PHONE

Guest Name

_____

Wishes & Messages

_____

_____

_____

_____

_____

_____

_____

Email/Phone

Guest Name

_____

Wishes & Messages

_____

_____

_____

_____

_____

_____

_____

Email/Phone

Guest Name

_____

Wishes & Messages

_____

_____

_____

_____

_____

_____

_____

Email/Phone

Guest Name

_____

Wishes & Messages

_____

_____

_____

_____

_____

_____

EMAIL/PHONE

Guest Name

_____

Wishes & Messages

_____

_____

_____

_____

_____

_____

✉ E

Email/Phone

Guest Name

_____

Wishes & Messages

_____

_____

_____

_____

_____

_____

_____

Email/Phone

Guest Name

_____

Wishes & Messages

_____

_____

_____

_____

_____

_____

_____

Email/Phone

Guest Name

_____

Wishes & Messages

_____

_____

_____

_____

_____

_____

_____

Email/Phone

Guest Name

_____

Wishes & Messages

_____

_____

_____

_____

_____

_____

Email/Phone

Guest Name

_____

Wishes & Messages

_____

_____

_____

_____

_____

_____

✉ E

Email/Phone

Guest Name

_____

Wishes & Messages

_____

_____

_____

_____

_____

_____

_____

Email/Phone

Guest Name

_____

Wishes & Messages

_____

_____

_____

_____

_____

_____

_____

EMAIL/PHONE

Guest Name

_____

Wishes & Messages

_____

_____

_____

_____

_____

_____

_____

✉ E

Email/Phone

Guest Name

_____

Wishes & Messages

_____

_____

_____

_____

_____

_____

EMAIL/PHONE

Guest Name

_____

Wishes & Messages

_____

_____

_____

_____

_____

_____

_____

✉ E

Email/Phone

Guest Name

_____

Wishes & Messages

_____

_____

_____

_____

_____

_____

EMAIL/PHONE

Guest Name

_____

Wishes & Messages

_____

_____

_____

_____

_____

_____

_____

✉ Email/Phone

Guest Name

_____

Wishes & Messages

_____

_____

_____

_____

_____

_____

EMAIL/PHONE

Guest Name

_____

Wishes & Messages

_____

_____

_____

_____

_____

_____

_____

Email/Phone

Guest Name

_____

Wishes & Messages

_____

_____

_____

_____

_____

_____

_____

✉ Email/Phone

Guest Name

_____

Wishes & Messages

_____

_____

_____

_____

_____

_____

_____

Email/Phone

Guest Name

_____

Wishes & Messages

_____

_____

_____

_____

_____

_____

EMAIL/PHONE

Guest Name

Wishes & Messages

_____

_____

_____

_____

_____

_____

_____

Email/Phone

Guest Name

_____

Wishes & Messages

_____

_____

_____

_____

_____

_____

Email/Phone

Guest Name

_____

Wishes & Messages

_____

_____

_____

_____

_____

_____

✉ E

EMAIL/PHONE

Guest Name

_____

Wishes & Messages

_____

_____

_____

_____

_____

_____

✉ E
Email/Phone

Guest Name

_____

Wishes & Messages

_____

_____

_____

_____

_____

_____

_____

EMAIL/PHONE

Guest Name

_____

Wishes & Messages

_____

_____

_____

_____

_____

_____

✉️
EMAIL/PHONE

Guest Name

_____

Wishes & Messages

_____

_____

_____

_____

_____

_____

_____

✉ E

EMAIL/PHONE

Guest Name

_____

Wishes & Messages

_____

_____

_____

_____

_____

_____

_____

Email/Phone

Guest Name

_____

Wishes & Messages

_____

_____

_____

_____

_____

_____

✉ E

Email/Phone

Guest Name

_____

Wishes & Messages

_____

_____

_____

_____

_____

_____

_____

EMAIL/PHONE

Guest Name

_____

Wishes & Messages

_____

_____

_____

_____

_____

_____

_____

EMAIL/PHONE

Guest Name

_____

Wishes & Messages

_____

_____

_____

_____

_____

_____

_____

EMAIL/PHONE

Guest Name

Wishes & Messages

_____

_____

_____

_____

_____

_____

_____

Email/Phone

Guest Name

_____

Wishes & Messages

_____

_____

_____

_____

_____

_____

_____

EMAIL/PHONE

Guest Name

_____

Wishes & Messages

_____

_____

_____

_____

_____

_____

_____

EMAIL/PHONE

Guest Name

_____

Wishes & Messages

_____

_____

_____

_____

_____

_____

Email/Phone

Guest Name

_____

Wishes & Messages

_____

_____

_____

_____

_____

_____

Email/Phone

Guest Name

_____

Wishes & Messages

_____

_____

_____

_____

_____

_____

Email/Phone

Guest Name

_____

Wishes & Messages

_____

_____

_____

_____

_____

_____

_____

EMAIL/PHONE

Guest Name

_____

Wishes & Messages

_____

_____

_____

_____

_____

_____

_____

✉ E

Email/Phone

Guest Name

_____

Wishes & Messages

_____

_____

_____

_____

_____

_____

_____

Email/Phone

Guest Name

_____

Wishes & Messages

_____

_____

_____

_____

_____

_____

_____

EMAIL/PHONE

Guest Name

_____

Wishes & Messages

_____

_____

_____

_____

_____

_____

_____

📧
Email/Phone

Guest Name

_____

Wishes & Messages

_____

_____

_____

_____

_____

_____

_____

EMAIL/PHONE

Guest Name

_____

Wishes & Messages

_____

_____

_____

_____

_____

_____

_____

Email/Phone

Guest Name

_____

Wishes & Messages

_____

_____

_____

_____

_____

_____

✉ **Email/Phone**

Guest Name

_____

Wishes & Messages

_____

_____

_____

_____

_____

_____

_____

✉ Email/Phone

Guest Name

_____

Wishes & Messages

_____

_____

_____

_____

_____

_____

EMAIL/PHONE

Guest Name

_____

Wishes & Messages

_____

_____

_____

_____

_____

_____

_____

Email/Phone

Guest Name

_____

Wishes & Messages

_____

_____

_____

_____

_____

_____

_____

EMAIL/PHONE

Guest Name

_____

Wishes & Messages

_____

_____

_____

_____

_____

_____

_____

EMAIL/PHONE

Guest Name

_____

Wishes & Messages

_____

_____

_____

_____

_____

_____

_____

Email/Phone

Guest Name

_____

Wishes & Messages

_____

_____

_____

_____

_____

_____

Email/Phone

Guest Name

_____

Wishes & Messages

_____

_____

_____

_____

_____

_____

_____

Email/Phone

Guest Name

_____

Wishes & Messages

_____

_____

_____

_____

_____

_____

_____

📧
Email/Phone

Guest Name

_____

Wishes & Messages

_____

_____

_____

_____

_____

_____

Email/Phone

Guest Name

_____

Wishes & Messages

_____

_____

_____

_____

_____

_____

_____

✉ E
EMAIL/PHONE

Guest Name

Wishes & Messages

_____

_____

_____

_____

_____

_____

_____

EMAIL/PHONE

Guest Name

_____

Wishes & Messages

_____

_____

_____

_____

_____

_____

_____

EMAIL/PHONE

Guest Name

_____

Wishes & Messages

_____

_____

_____

_____

_____

_____

Email/Phone

Guest Name

_____

Wishes & Messages

_____

_____

_____

_____

_____

_____

Email/Phone

Guest Name

_____

Wishes & Messages

_____

_____

_____

_____

_____

_____

_____

Email/Phone

Guest Name

_____

Wishes & Messages

_____

_____

_____

_____

_____

_____

_____

✉ E

EMAIL/PHONE

Guest Name

_____

Wishes & Messages

_____

_____

_____

_____

_____

_____

_____

Email/Phone

Guest Name

Wishes & Messages

_____

_____

_____

_____

_____

_____

_____

EMAIL/PHONE

Guest Name

Wishes & Messages

Email/Phone

Guest Name

_____

Wishes & Messages

_____

_____

_____

_____

_____

_____

_____

EMAIL/PHONE

Guest Name

_____

Wishes & Messages

_____

_____

_____

_____

_____

_____

✉ E

Email/Phone

Guest Name

_____

Wishes & Messages

_____

_____

_____

_____

_____

_____

_____

Email/Phone

Guest Name

_____

Wishes & Messages

_____

_____

_____

_____

_____

_____

EMAIL/PHONE

Guest Name

_____

Wishes & Messages

_____

_____

_____

_____

_____

_____

_____

Email/Phone

Guest Name

_____

Wishes & Messages

_____

_____

_____

_____

_____

_____

_____

Email/Phone

Guest Name

_____

Wishes & Messages

_____

_____

_____

_____

_____

_____

EMAIL/PHONE

Guest Name

Wishes & Messages

_____

_____

_____

_____

_____

_____

_____

Email/Phone

Guest Name

_____

Wishes & Messages

_____

_____

_____

_____

_____

_____

_____

Email/Phone

Guest Name

_____

Wishes & Messages

_____

_____

_____

_____

_____

_____

_____

Email/Phone

Guest Name

_____

Wishes & Messages

_____

_____

_____

_____

_____

_____

_____

EMAIL/PHONE

Guest Name

_____

Wishes & Messages

_____

_____

_____

_____

_____

_____

✉ Email/Phone

Guest Name

_____

Wishes & Messages

_____

_____

_____

_____

_____

_____

_____

✉ E

Email/Phone

Guest Name

_____

Wishes & Messages

_____

_____

_____

_____

_____

_____

✉ Email/Phone

Guest Name

_____

Wishes & Messages

_____

_____

_____

_____

_____

_____

_____

✉ E

EMAIL/PHONE

Guest Name

_____

Wishes & Messages

_____

_____

_____

_____

_____

_____

Email/Phone

Guest Name

_____

Wishes & Messages

_____

_____

_____

_____

_____

_____

✉ E

EMAIL/PHONE

NOTES & PHOTOS

NOTES & PHOTOS

NOTES & PHOTOS

NOTES & PHOTOS

NOTES & PHOTOS

GIFT LOG

Name / Email / Phone	Gift

GIFT LOG

Name / Email / Phone	Gift

GIFT LOG

Name / Email / Phone	Gift

GIFT LOG

Name /Email /Phone	Gift

GIFT LOG

Name / Email / Phone	Gift

GIFT LOG

Name / Email / Phone	Gift

GIFT LOG

Name / Email / Phone	Gift